Buckland-in-the-Moor: A
of the Parish &

Buckland-in-the-Moor is just one of a number of Bucklands in Devon, all of which take their name from *book land*, meaning land held by Charter (or *book*). The ancient Manor is named as Bochelande in Domesday, the name probably originating from the time when its lands were held by the Bishop of Crediton prior to the 11th century. In the 13th century much of its land was again held under Charter, having been granted to Torre Abbey by a descendant of the Roger de Bokelande, who held the Manor in 1086. A dozen or so of these earlier Covenants survive, and in them are found some early forms of the names of some of the farms which still exist in the parish at the present day.

Radeclyve (Ruddycleave) and Suthbrok (Southbrook) are mentioned in the Charters, and Chiempabere (Challamoor) is also known to have existed before the Conquest. Stone Farm, too, has ancient origins, owned by William atte Stone in 1330. At around this time Sir John L'Ercedekne succeeded the Bokelandes as owner of most of the rest of Buckland, either through purchase or inheritance.

Much of the mid to late Medieval history of the Manor itself has been lost in the mists of time. By the 14th century Buckland had apparently become part of the Manor of Stoke-in-Teignhead, although at the time of the Dissolution it was part of Wolborrow Manor. By the late 16th century the Manor had become independent again, and in 1578 was sold by Thomas Carewe to Raphe Woodleigh, the latter family only holding it for a short time before selling out to the Bastard family in 1614.

The Bastards, who were Lords of the Manor for the following three centuries, were themselves an ancient family, and a book published in Paris in 1848 entitled *Généalogie de la Maison de Bastard* traces the pedigree of the name through Rahier, Lord of Bastardiéne-sur-Sèvre in 1040, back to Rivallon, Count of Poher in Cornwall c850. One of the sons of the Bastardiéne line, Robert, was among the Breton followers of Alain Fargent, who sailed with William of Normandy in 1066, and after the Conquest he settled in Devon.

Regarding industries, it is not improbable that tin streaming on a minor scale along the Ruddycleave dates from the 12th or 13th centuries, and sites in Awsewell Woods (just over the border in Ashburton parish, but still part of the Buckland Estate) may also be of some antiquity, but there are no definite records of mineral working until the late 16th century. The woollen industry is possibly as old as the tinning industry, and there was also a corn mill at Bridge as early as the 13th century. The timber plantations have also formed an important part of the Estate from the earliest times, and it is likely that many of "Englande's mightie oakes" from the Buckland woods went to Dartmouth to build the ships of the line which routed Villeneuve's fleet at Trafalgar. Extensive areas of the woodland were also used for charcoal burning.

The first mention of the church is to be found in Bishop Lacey's Register of 1420, but the first church on the site was probably erected in the 12th century. Like many of the churches in the smaller Dartmoor parishes, it first strikes one as being a little spartan inside, with no major memorials or tombs, yet it has a "homely" feel about it and boasts a 12th century font as well as a 15th century screen, which originates from Bradninch Church. The unique clock face on the tower – containing an inscription which reads 'MY DEAR MOTHER' instead of the usual numerals (a memorial to one of the Whitley family of nearby Buckland Court) – is one of its striking features (forgive the unintended pun!), and it is one of only a dozen or so churches in the county which still retains some medieval floor tiles in the nave. The little tower, typical of the Dartmoor churches, houses a peal of eight bells. The earliest Churchwardens' Accounts date from 1635 and reveal much of interest about parish life in the mid to late 17th century. The surviving Registers begin c1624.

St. Peter's Church. Note the clock face containing the inscription 'MY DEAR MOTHER'.

4

A Walk Around the Parish

As the post-Medieval history of the little parish of Buckland-in-the-Moor is inextricably linked to the history of the Manor, which to all intents and purposes are one and the same, the most appropriate place to begin is in the church. Here, in the floor of the north aisle, will be found the black Ashburton marble tombstone of Raphe Woodleigh, who died in 1593, the first Lord of the Manor to be buried in St Peter's Church, Buckland. This tombstone is the oldest dated floor ledger to be found in any Dartmoor church.

From the church, head for the rear gate of the churchyard beside the Church House. Here the Layman family lived in the mid 17th century, one of whom, Walter, was paid from the Churchwardens' Accounts for "the tuneing of psalms" for a number of years in the 1660/70s. During the Commonwealth period the playing of musical instruments during church services was banned, and these payments probably indicate the first time that singing in St Peter's had been accompanied since before the Civil War. The instrument he played was probably a bass viol.

Before continuing, notice the broken cross head which is cemented onto the top of the wall to the left of the gate. This cross probably once stood on the pedestal where now stands the large oak tree planted in 1935 to mark the Jubilee of King George V. On the pedestal base is a tablet with a now very weathered inscription which commemorates this event, and the telegrams sent to and from Buckingham Palace at that time may be seen inside the church.

The rear of the old Church House, backing onto the graveyard.

5

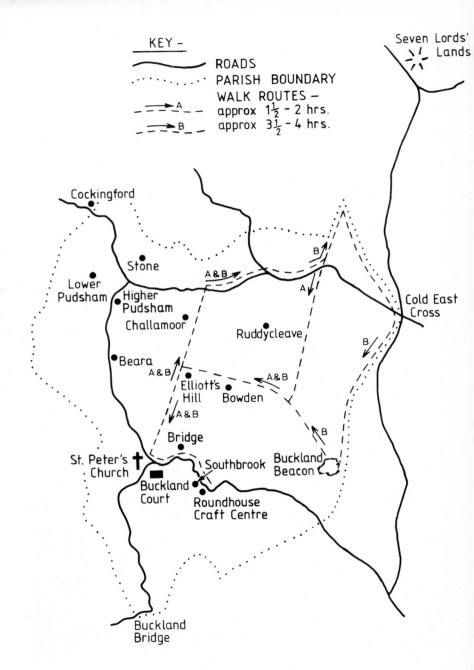

KEY -

ROADS
PARISH BOUNDARY
WALK ROUTES -
A — approx 1½ - 2 hrs.
B — approx 3½ - 4 hrs.

Seven Lords' Lands

Cockingford

Stone

Lower Pudsham

Higher Pudsham

Challamoor

A & B

Ruddycleave

Cold East Cross

Beara

A & B

Elliott's Hill

Bowden

A & B

A & B

St. Peter's Church

Bridge

Southbrook

Buckland Beacon

Buckland Court

Roundhouse Craft Centre

Buckland Bridge

THE PARISH OF BUCKLAND - IN - THE - MOOR

6

The Smerdons of Elliott's Hill

On leaving the oak tree, turn left up the road past the church and immediately right opposite the lay-by, up the lane called Elliott's Hill, pausing momentarily to see another tree and an inscribed plaque on the grassy verge; this records the Jubilee of our present Queen. Further up is Elliott's Hill Farm, from which the lane takes its name.

In 1639, the year after the great storm at neighbouring Widecombe, Richard Smerdon and his wife Christian became the Manor's tenants at this farm, and little did they then realise that from them would rise a dynasty which would dominate the little community in Buckland for nearly three centuries. This family retained their hold on this little piece of Dartmoor until late Victorian times, and an unbroken line of Smerdons can be traced as occupiers of the farm through nine consecutive generations until the death of James Smerdon in 1886. The names and periods of tenure of every one of them is now known: the first six generations, fathers and sons, were all named Richard!

Smerdons also reigned supreme as the senior Buckland tenant-occupiers throughout this period, and at one stage, during the mid 18th century, descendants of the Elliott's Hill line had spread to hold virtually the entire leasehold property on the Manorial Estate, aside from the cottages and the mills. Their fall from this apparently unassailable position as the leading Buckland family, however, was sudden and dramatic, and came about as the mid-Victorian agricultural depression tightened its grip on the parish, which led to the younger generations slowly drifting away from the land, turning, instead, to seek their fortunes in the towns and cities. Thus, following the death of James in 1886, there was not one Smerdon as a tenant at any property within the entire parish, so Elliott's Hill, which was the home of the first members of this well known Dartmoor family name to settle in Buckland, was, fittingly perhaps, also the home of the last of them.

Turning aside from the little farmstead, where so much of Buckland's post-Medieval history was written, continue up the lane and pause where a large stone protrudes from the hedgerow opposite a field gate of Ruddycleave Farm. This is a traditional granite gatehanger stone, and on its underside can be seen the pivot hole which would have taken the upright stanchion of the wooden gate. There are a number of similar stones which may be seen scattered around the Dartmoor lanes and byways, but there is only one which is still in use, and which is well worth a visit; this is at Coxtor Farm in Peter Tavy parish. Returning to the one here near Ruddycleave, this farm underwent an extensive renovation during the 1760s, and one entry in the accounts of these repairs records the payment of a shilling (5p) for "three hangers for gates". Perhaps this stone may have been one of those gatehangers.

The Manor Pound

Further on again, beyond a ruinous gate entrance near the side track to Ruddycleave, the lane widens into a now very overgrown elongated triangular piece of ground. This enclosed area, there is good reason to believe, may have been the former Manor Pound: there is evidence that a Pound once existed, for in the Manor Court Rolls of 1686 it was recorded that its walls were in a state of disrepair, but that it was at this site is inferred more from the lack of any other suitable location within the parish rather than any firm proof. That livestock pounds need not have been purpose-built enclosures in the conventional sense (such as that at Dunnabridge) is illustrated by the fact that those at Creber and Thornworthy, on the edge of high Dartmoor, are themselves merely irregular pieces of ground enclosed between newtake walls.

And there is one piece of evidence which lends support to the idea that this was the ancient Manor Pound, and this is to be found when you emerge onto the road via the gate at the head of this area of rough ground; a tall dressed granite pillar, the sole survivor of the original pair which once stood here. Look at it closely, for it is of exactly the same dimensions and design as the pair which still stand at the head of Buckland Drive, which was formerly the rear entrance to the Manor House of Buckland Court, and which you will be able to see when you return to the church. There seems to be no other reason for having pillars of this style at the head of what would otherwise be an ordinary farm track, than to form a more imposing entrance to the Manor Pound. And the site is, in fact, ideally placed: as can be seen, the gate opens straight onto Pudsham Down, so gives direct access to the pastures there; it is also easily accessible for driving livestock off Buckland Common via Ripman's Gate and Bowden Lane and on up the lane along which you have just walked. You will pass through Ripman's Gate later in the walk.

Turning right along the road across Pudsham Down, you will soon descend to the small bridge over the Ruddycleave Brook. This was formerly the Mill Brook, a name which it took from the mill at the tiny hamlet of Bridge, which was in existence at least as early as the 13th century, if not before. No bridge was here at that early date, and the site, instead, was named as Juhelisforde in 13th century Charters which bequeathed land to Torre Abbey, a name which survived, in a corrupted form, until well into the 19th century when Pudsham Down was often still referred to as Giles Down; that Giles was a derivation of the earlier name Juhelis seems certain.

Ruddycleave Farm

After crossing the bridge you have a choice of two routes. The shorter one is to turn right along the wide grassy track which will lead you to Ripman's Gate. This pleasant walk provides a splendid view of the fine spread of Ruddycleave Farm across the valley, and its magnificent medieval longhouse. The farm has an interesting and rather unusual history. Sometime during the Medieval period it was bequeathed to the parish so that its rent could provide for the upkeep of the church and its related expenses, and its unique position within the Buckland community gave rise to a rather bizarre situation in later centuries.

Brief mention has already been made of the fact that during the immediate post-Dissolution period, following the end of Torre Abbey's controlling interests, Buckland became part of the Manor of Wolborrow. The latter was also formerly part of the Torre Abbey Estate, and at some now undefined period Ruddycleave had become incorporated with that Manor, the precise reasons for which have been lost. It had long been the custom that tenants would owe Suit of Court to the Manor and be obliged to attend the Manor Courts and perform certain duties for the Manorial Lord. Freeholders within the domain of the Manor were similarly obligated towards it. In the late 15th century Buckland Manor was sold and once again became an independent Manor in its own right, and it was this which gave rise to the strange situation that was to emerge.

For Ruddycleave, which had long been freehold (inasmuch that it was effectively owned by the church and not the Manor), could not be sold with the rest of Buckland due to its independent status. This single farm, rather oddly, thus became an isolated outlier of Wolborrow Manor, and the performance of Suit of Court to the latter was still being undertaken by Buckland Churchwardens at least until the end of the 17th century (this situation, although an unusual one was, incidentally, by no means unique: Sortridge Manor in Sampford Spiney parish on Western Dartmoor was at one stage in its history an isolated outlier of Peter Tavy).

Continuing along the grassy track will soon bring you to Ripman's Gate at the head of Bowden Lane. Here the description of the shorter route will pause momentarily so as to allow the longer route from Ruddycleave Bridge to be described first, for this will also later return you to Ripman's Gate (see page 15)

The longer route from Ruddycleave Bridge: To participate in this longer route from Ruddycleave Bridge, turn left along the narrow track which leads upstream along the left bank of the brook and continue until you reach the main gravel and dirt track near Blackslade Ford. All along the route you will notice that the banks of the stream are marked with low spoil heaps of stones and scarred with shallow furrows. These features mark the tin-streaming activities which were carried out along the Ruddycleave in Medieval times. Perhaps this was the site of the Whitta Pitte workings named by Raphe Woodleigh, Lord of the Manor, in his will dated 1593.

The wider gravel track, which you will shortly reach, is known as the Tunhill Road, the ancient pack-horse track leading from the farm of that name towards Cold East Cross and the main Chagford-Ashburton highway. Directly ahead are the frontier heights of Dartmoor – Rippon Tor, the highest of the Hey Tor group, Saddle Tor behind and hiding Hey Tor itself, Pil Tor and Top Tor slightly to your left. If you are here on a sunny afternoon in late summer or early autumn the slope rising to Pil Tor will be ablaze with the purple and yellow hues of heather and gorse.

The Halter Path and a late 18th Century Boundary Dispute

Turning to the left, you should find it easy to cross the shallow ford. If not, then you can still see the main feature of interest from the left bank. This is the wall which runs at right angles to the enclosure on the flank of Whittaburrow, where there is a gate entrance astride the track, and continues to the edge of the brook. You will notice that here the wall abruptly ends; there are a few stones lying in the bed of the brook, but on the left bank the wall has been totally destroyed, only the faint outlines of its former course being visible as low overgrown mounds of collapsed stones.

This wall is of particular significance in relation to a boundary dispute which arose in 1771, for its builders, the Woodley family of neighbouring Halsanger Manor, had erected it across the ancient route known as the Halter Path. This is the grassy track which you have just been following, a continuation of the track from Ripman's Gate and the route which by ancient custom had been used by the Lords of the Manor of Buckland to attend open air meet-

The open moor above Blackslade Ford; part of the wall involved in the Boundary Dispute is visible, with Pil Tor on the skyline beyond.

ings at the cairn known as Seven Lords' Lands (this cairn may still be seen today: it is clearly marked on the map, near Hemsworthy Gate, just a short distance outside the Buckland parish boundary).

The Lord of Buckland, Pollexfen Bastard, initiated proceedings against the Woodleys with the result that the latter were ordered to destroy the wall and were bound over in the sum of £200 to abide by the decision of the arbitrators. Hence the reason why the wall on the left bank of the brook, which blocked the Halter Path, is now totally ruinous, in stark contrast to the other section which still stands and remains in reasonably good condition to this day. Upstream of the Tunhill Road the original route of the Halter Path has been lost to the encroaching mires, but faint vestiges of a track may be picked out in the vicinity of the ruined wall. There is another, very much longer, section of partly ruined wall running up this side of the brook, which above the ford bears the name Blackslade Water: this section of the wall was allowed to remain in place under the terms of the 1771 arbitration for it did not interfere with the Lord of Buckland's right of way along the ancient path.

The Bounds of the Manor

By continuing along the Tunhill Road with Rippon Tor to your left, you will very soon come to a boundary stone standing on a ruined cairn beside the track. This stands beside the longer section of walling which curves round and begins to peter out further upslope. The now very ruinous cairn has, like the

The Crooked Stone beside the Tunhill Track. In the background are Pil Tor and Top Tor.

others you will see along this line, been a bondmark of the Manor of Buckland for many centuries; in 1593 it was named Culverburrough, a name it retained for many years until 1837, when it was changed to Buiscate Burrow. Later in that year the present bondstone was erected on the spot, together with most of the others along the eastern border of the Manor, and these bear the inscription 'EPB 1837/A/B'. The letters denote Edmund Pollexfen Bastard, Lord of the Manor of Buckland in the year in which they were set up, and the parishes of Ashburton and Buckland. Mention was made earlier that the parish and Manor are to all intents and purposes one and the same, and the extent of the Manor of Buckland is exactly that of the tiny parish; the stones, known locally as the A–B Stones, thus mark the limits of both Manor and parish.

Continuing along the track, the second stone (a little way off the track, to your left) is, as its appearance immediately suggests, very much older and bears only the letters 'A/B', although they are much larger and more crudely cut. This ancient bondmark was known as the Crooked Stone in 1613, and if you turn about and look at the 'A' side of the stone you can clearly see the reason for it being so called. In 1837 the spot was named Bun Burrow.

The third stone, a considerably taller pillar, is also marked only with the parish letters, but is a much more modern stone. This stands on a very small ruinous cairn remnant, and it was, in fact, this fairly insignificant pile which enabled the rest of the ancient bondmarks to be accurately identified and correlated over a period of some four centuries. For here the line of the boundary changes very slightly, a fact which was remarked upon in a 1837 survey, which also named the spot as Penny Pie Burrow. Fortunately, this name had been retained virtually unchanged since 1593, being variously spelt Pony Poole, Pennypowls, Penny Poole, and Penny Pole Burrough or Burrow through seven boundary reviews, and the fact that the name could be positively identified with an exact location also allowed the rest of the bondmarks on either side to be placed in their correct sequence and positions.

The fourth stone, whilst another of the standard A–B stones, is not on an ancient bondmark, but the fifth is another "odd one out", a tall pillar bearing the inscription 'PW 1746'. That the letters refer to Peter Woodley, Lord of Halsanger Manor, is certain. But the reason for the date remains something of a mystery as a stone stood at the spot much earlier, a "longstone near Chagford Way" being named in a boundary report of 1683. (Chagford Way obviously refers to the main Ashburton-Chagford highway, then merely a dirt track but still an important route for commerce in the Dartmoor borderlands of these early centuries. Consequently, there must have been a tall pillar – a "longstone" – standing at this spot at least as early as 1683).

The final stone in this direction stands at Cold East Cross, a spot which was named as Horeburrough in 1593 and developed, through various alternative spellings, to become the Ham Burrow of 1837. This last name can again be firmly allocated to this spot, for the reference to it also mentions the road.

As you turn around to your right from the junction and begin to make your way uphill you will shortly see the seventh stone in the series leading towards Buckland Beacon. This sets you on the correct course for the next part of the route, and you should continue by passing the stone and a number of other A–B stones until you reach the last, erected upon a site which, in 1837, was named Hurrah Burrow. After this point the surveyors directed that the boundary went "thence in a southerly direction to a stone by the fence wall", and this tiny apology for a bondstone does, in fact, still stand to this day, right at the corner of the wall which is now directly ahead of you.

The rocks of Buckland Beacon are now in sight and, continuing upslope with the wall to your left, you will pass the sites named as Wolstorrburrough or Two Burroughs, and Greenway Head or One Burrough. These were also once large cairns, but they have been robbed of their stones for the building of the newtake wall, although they can still be picked out on the ground with a little difficulty: the first site is a large patch of small stones where the wall bends slightly, and the next is a low grassy mound near the crest of the hill, almost alongside the highest of two hunt gates in the wall. That this last is indeed the ancient bondmark is affirmed by the fact that the 1613 report stated that it was next to a "little path from Wolstorr", a path which can still be traced leading through the gate; the former location can be ascertained from the fact that archaeologists had earlier established the site of twin cairns near the bend in the wall, hence Two Burroughs.

Leave aside the Beacon Rocks for the moment and continue a little way downslope to a large upright slab standing beside the wall. For around one and a half centuries this has been known as the Grey Mare, and locals still refer to the stone by this name. However, research has now firmly established that the correct name for the stone is, in fact, Longstone, although the stone will doubtless retain its mistaken identity as the Grey Mare for many years to come.

The error arose following the building of the newtake wall in 1771 when the original Gray Mare, which stood a little further downslope next to the spring called Stidwell, was destroyed. Prior to this time two bond marks had always been named on this slope, the Longstone and the Gray Mare. The loss of one of these was highlighted by some confusion over the correctness of the names in the boundary review of 1837, an uncertainty which prompted the recorders to write of "a bound stone called the Gray Mare or where the Gray Mare formerly stood". By careful scrutiny of the full text of all the boundary reports, together with field work, it was established that it was, indeed, the Gray Mare which had been lost, a name which subsequently became mistakenly attached to the former Longstone.

Before leaving the subject of bondmarks, the ancient custom of Beating the Bounds should be briefly mentioned. Many parishes on Dartmoor (and elsewhere) continue the tradition to this day, during which it is customary that the youngest members of the community will be "bumped" on the bondstones in order to impress their location and names upon their memory. A full list of those who Beat the Bounds of the Manor in 1698 has survived, and from other documentary sources much can be learnt about them. Two of the party who attended that day in June three centuries ago were Richard Burnell junior and John Smerdon junior; both would have been around 3 or 4 years old at the time and would, doubtless, have been "bumped" on some of the bondmarks in the time-honoured tradition. John was one of the Smerdons of Elliott's Hill, who have already been mentioned; Richard would have been born in the great long-house at Bowden, which you will be able to see later on the walk.

The Ten Commandments Stones

You have now walked along virtually the entire eastern boundary of the Manor (only this section of the line is on public land), although you could if you wished continue down the steep descent to the road at Awsewell Corner where once stood the last bondmark on the Common, a stone called Throshell or Drossell Stone in earlier centuries; this stone, like the Gray Mare, no longer survives. Turning right along the road will bring you to the little hamlet of Buckland, which will be described later.

The route now described will take you back down to the church via Ripman's Gate, but whichever route you pursue do not neglect to at first visit the Beacon Rocks to see one of the most remarkable man-made features on Dartmoor. Well, not one, but two, in fact, for there are two huge slabs of granite resting on the shoulder of the rock outcrops, which bear the complete verses

Buckland Beacon and the Ten Commandments Stones.

of the Ten Commandments. The inscriptions were cut by W. Arthur Clements in 1928 at the behest of William Whitley, then Lord of the Manor, to commemorate the rejection by Parliament of the proposed New Book of Common Prayer. Whilst Clements was doing this work he camped in a small hut on the edge of the woods below the Beacon. Despite the fact that they were cut so recently, even after only fifty years or so the letters had become very weathered and barely legible under the onslaught of the winds and rains which are only too frequent on this eastern edge of Dartmoor. But they were recut in the summer of 1995 and are once again perfectly clear. Another inscription on the Beacon Rocks, which is to be found just above the Ten Commandments Stones, commemorates the Silver Jubilee of the King in 1935.

This hill, like many other prominent heights on Dartmoor, had been used as a beacon station for many centuries, when fires would be lit as part of a chain across the country, sometimes carrying warning messages, sometimes in celebration. Buckland Beacon doubtless carried many such warnings in former times, when enemy fleets were sighted off Plymouth, its fires flashing the messages to the coast around Dartmouth. Such is its prominence that no less than 47 other beacon fires could be seen from this summit during Queen Victoria's Jubilee celebrations in 1887. The most recent occasion on which a beacon fire was lit here was in 1995, on the 50th Anniversary of VE Day.

The Bowden Longhouse

Leaving the Beacon and its extensive views, turn right from your original line of ascent from Cold East Cross and continue downslope in the direction of Ruddycleave Farm in the valley below, with the rocks and the newtake wall behind you; there are a number of sheep tracks which you can follow. These will lead you down to Ripman's Gate, which, in the late 17th century, was known as Liddy Gate. Away to your right from the gate runs the Halter Path, part of which you have already walked along higher up the valley.

The shorter route, continued: Entering the stoney and rutted lane, pause for a moment beside the first field gate to your right to see the slotted gatepost standing in the entrance. Posts such as these, like the gatehanger you saw earlier, were the traditional methods of closing field entrances in former times, and in this case a pair of slotted posts would stand either side of the gate, the latter being formed by loose wooden poles dropped into the slots. There are a number of variations in the style used; this one contains tapered slots enabling the poles to be more securely held when rammed home. As with the gatehanger, some particulars survive regarding the making of gateposts: in 1876 one Thomas Egbeare was paid for "clifting" (cleaving) 17 gateposts for Bowden (these fields belong to the farm of that name), which were doubtless

The late medieval longhouse at Bowden; the oldest part of the range is on the higher side of the porch.

made to replace the older slotted gateposts, of which the one here is the sole survivor in the area.

Continue down the lane towards the little bridge over the Ruddycleave and, as you emerge from the shadow of the overhanging trees, a magnificent sight awaits you as the fine Bowden longhouse comes into full view. A late medieval granite rubble longhouse in the traditional Dartmoor style, with a half-hipped slate and thatch roof, this may have been built by the Woolcott family, who are known to have owned the farm during the latter half of the 16th century. The property came by marriage into the hands of the Jennynge family, who then sold it to Buckland Manor for £200 in 1639, and amongst the first of the Manor's tenants there was John Burnell whose grandson, Richard, has already been mentioned in relation to the Beating of the Bounds ceremony conducted in 1698. The Burnells retained their tenancy on the main tenement here, which included the longhouse, until the early 19th century, a period of tenure exceeded in Buckland only by the Smerdons of neighbouring Elliott's.

The farmstead, during these early centuries, was split into sub-tenements, and at one of the smaller ones at the time of the sale to the Manor was Thomas Endecott, who was paying an annual rent of just 6s 8d (approx 33p) for his smallholding. At the other tenement was Ralph Cater, who had only recently moved from Elliott's Hill, leaving the latter vacant for the Smerdons to move in and begin their long occupation at the latter farm. In later centuries there were Smerdons at Bowden as well, one them, Elias, going on to become the Lord of the Manor's gamekeeper at Kitley for thirty years; Kitley, near the Yealm Estuary, was the Manorial seat of the Bastard family (Lords of Buckland) from the late 17th century onwards.

As you climb the lane after admiring the longhouse and other buildings of Bowden, by looking over the hedge to your left you can also see some of the older buildings of Elliott's.

Once you reach the junction, turning to your left will bring you back to the church, and it is appropriate that your walk should end almost where it began, with a final visit to the churchyard. For near the small vestry building stands a tall cross which marks the last resting place of William Pollexfen Bastard of Kitley and Buckland Court, who died in 1915, only the second Lord of the Manor to be buried at St Peter's in over three centuries. He was one of the last of the Bastard line who had been Lords of the Manor for twelve generations since 1614, and was the only one of them to be buried in Buckland.

Before you continue downhill to the hamlet, remember to walk along the Buckland Drive a short distance (turn right out of the rear churchyard gate) to have a look at the granite pillars and compare their design to that which you saw earlier at the gate leading to the probable site of the Manor Pound.

A Picture-Postcard Scene

Returning to the Church House, turn right and descend the steep hill to the tiny hamlet of Buckland-in-the-Moor. The old Manor House of Buckland Court is on your right as you descend, hiding behind the imposing and now crumbling and unkempt granite walls; it is on private ground and cannot be visited and, regrettably, cannot even be seen.

The little hamlet at Bridge, with its picture-postcard cottages, epitomises the Dartmoor village scene and needs no introduction here; it is world famous and, with the possible exception of Hey Tor, its romantically situated cluster of whitewash and thatched cottages is the most photographed scene on the whole of Dartmoor.

It is interesting to pause and reflect that little cottages such as these were originally built for the labourers on the Estate. Their names are revealed through the pages of some of the wages books which survive. Joshua Lear lived in one of these for nearly fifty years until he died in 1878, his years as old as the century itself. One of his neighbours during much of this period was William Callaway, who had lived in his cottage for around thirty years until he died in 1871; another was William Coneybear, who, in the 1881 Census, still described himself as a farm labourer (and not, you will note, as a "retired" farm labourer) — he was then 81 years old! That he was indeed probably still working despite his great age is proved by the case of Joshua Lear already mentioned: he was still working in the timber plantations the year before he died, earning just 1s 10d (approx 9p) per day.

The cottages at the tiny hamlet of Bridge.

There were once two mills here, one on either side of the little brook. The earliest, the corn or grist mill, has already been mentioned in connection with the ancient name of the stream; this once stood on the left as you look at the scene. On the opposite bank was a tucking, or fulling, mill (a woollen mill) of unknown antiquity; the first mention of this is found in a lease of 1612 when John Stonier took over as the tenant, but it may have been in existence long before that time. Neither of these buildings survives today. The tucking mill fell into disrepair when it was left vacant sometime in the early 1690s, and was demolished at around the turn of the century, evidence of which exists in the terms of the lease on a neighbouring property. The corn mill was destroyed by fire sometime during the early decades of the 18th century, and at around the same period it is known that one of the cottages also had to be rebuilt. No doubt a cottage had accidentally caught fire, and the conflagration had swept quickly through the compact group of thatched buildings in the hamlet.

The grist mill was actually rebuilt in 1741, when one George Coneybear took on the lease after having agreed to finance the repairs himself. The terms of his lease record these facts, and that he had been at "great expense": the total expenditure for a complete rebuild, together with all the necessary equipment for the operation of the mill and the cutting of a new leat, cost him the princely sum of just £30! The building, which to this day stands on the spot, probably utilises the shell of the older one for, although it was probably gutted, the accounts of the work undertaken in the rebuilding indicate that it was not completely razed to the ground.

If you can bring yourself to turn away from this charming scene, continue along the road until you reach Southbrook. The view which greets you is a complete contrast to the scene you have just left, but is nonetheless attractive in its own way, its imposing and sturdy grey granite ashlar walls and the magnificent roundhouse typical of a large working Dartmoor farm. This, like Bowden, was also sub-divided into separate tenements in former times. Smerdons were here as well, of course, and three or four successive generations held the combined spread of the largest of the Southbrook tenements and the Court Barton fields, which, at the time, was the largest leasehold property in the parish. During the early years of the 19th century this, like Bowden and some of the other farms on the Estate, became unified into single farms. It may surprise you to learn that there was also once a little school at Southbrook; in the 1880s there were just 12 children there.

Notice the large granite trough and lipstone opposite the entrance to Southbrook as you pass, and the agricultural implements outside the main feature of the building from which the Roundhouse Craft Centre takes its name. The Centre, which should certainly be included on your list of places to visit whilst in Buckland, also offers a range of refreshments to revitalise you following your walk — and to prepare you for the short but stiff climb back up to the church!

As an alternative return route, and a contrast to the open moorland over

The Roundhouse Craft Centre.

19

which you earlier walked, there is a pleasant woodland walk alongside the Ruddycleave Brook through the Woodland Trust-owned part of the Estate, the entrance gate to which is opposite the cottages at Bridge. A choice of two circular routes along narrow paths will lead you to the road which climbs up from the Lower Buckland Lodges. Upon emerging onto this, turn right, and in a short distance you will arrive back at the church.

✳ ✳ ✳ ✳ ✳

Acknowledgements

My thanks are due to Paul Brough, John Fell, Anne Morgan, Diane Roper and Emma West at the West Devon Record Office, Plymouth, and to Ann Landers, and staff at the Plymouth Central Library Local Studies Dept for their assistance in searching out documentary and other sources, and to Dave & Kath Brewer for information on the Manor/Parish Bounds. The archive material which has been consulted is held at the West Devon Record Office, and a full listing of all Buckland Manor & Parish documents is available there.

A catalogue record for this book is available from the British Library

Published by Ladybird Books Ltd
A Penguin Company
Penguin Books Ltd, 80 Strand, London WC2R 0RL, UK
Penguin Books Australia Ltd, Camberwell, Victoria, Australia
Penguin Books (NZ) Ltd, Cnr Airbourne and Rosedale Roads, Albany, Auckland, 1310, New Zealand

1 3 5 7 9 10 8 6 4 2

Printed in China

The
Christmas Story

Retold by Hilary Ayling
and Keith Munro
Edited by Marie Birkinshaw
Illustrated by Mark Robertson

Ladybird

— ☆ —

$\mathcal{M}$ary was thinking about her wedding. A few weeks ago, Joseph the carpenter had asked her to marry him, and she was very happy.

As Mary stood, the whole room suddenly filled with light.

"Ah, the sun has come out at last!" thought Mary.

But the bright light wasn't the sun, and what Mary saw made her drop down to her knees – she was so afraid.

— ☆ —

Standing before Mary was an angel. He was wearing white robes that glowed and his skin seemed to shine like gold.

"Don't be afraid," said the angel. "My name is Gabriel and God has sent me to give you a special message. You are going to have a baby who will be God's own son. You are to call him Jesus."

Mary thought for a moment. Then she said, "I will do whatever God wants."

That night, the angel Gabriel also visited Joseph in a dream to give him the news. When Joseph awoke he was very surprised, but agreed to look after the baby Jesus.

The months passed, and the Roman Emperor gave the order for a census. Everyone had to return to the place where they had first been born. There, they would all be counted.

Now, Joseph's birthplace was the town of Bethlehem, and that was a very long way from Nazareth where Mary and Joseph lived.

They packed some blankets, warm clothes and food for their journey.

Joseph led Mary on the donkey for many days and nights until they finally arrived at Bethlehem.

When Mary and Joseph arrived in Bethlehem, they knocked on the door of every inn in town, but there was no room.

Just as Mary and Joseph were about to give up hope, the innkeeper at the last hotel offered them shelter in his stable where the animals slept. It was warm and dry, and Joseph put the blankets down on some clean straw to make a soft bed.

That night, the baby was born. Mary and Joseph called him Jesus as Gabriel had said.

— ☆ —

Away on the hills outside Bethlehem, some shepherds were taking care of their sheep.

Suddenly, they realised that the sky was getting brighter and brighter.

"What's happening?" shouted one of the frightened shepherds.

But then the angel Gabriel spoke. "Don't be afraid! I bring good news. Today, God's own son has been born in Bethlehem. You will find him in a stable, lying in a manger."

Then, the whole sky was filled with a choir of singing angels.

— ☆ —

The shepherds felt excited! They weren't afraid any more.

As soon as the angels had gone, they rushed off to Bethlehem to find the baby Jesus.

When the shepherds arrived at the stable, they saw the baby Jesus lying in a manger.

They were happy because everything was just as the angel Gabriel had said it would be.

Far away in Jerusalem, some important travellers had arrived at King Herod's palace. These were wise men who studied the stars.

Their books had told them the meaning of a new star. It was a sign that a special baby had been born who would one day be a great king. They had gone to Herod's palace hoping to find him. But there was no baby there.

When King Herod heard their tale he was worried. He hated the thought of anyone being king but himself.

Still, he told them to go to Bethlehem. "When you have found the new king, come and tell me where he is, so I can go and worship him too," he lied.

So the wise men went on to Bethlehem, following the star that stood still in the sky – right over the place where Jesus was.

When they saw him, they knelt down to worship, and give him their precious gifts of gold, frankincense and myrrh.

That night, in their dreams, God told the wise men not to go back to King Herod. So they set out on the long journey home by a different route.

Joseph, Mary and the baby stayed in Bethlehem until one night when the angel Gabriel visited Joseph with a message.

"Get up!" said Gabriel. "King Herod has heard that Jesus has been born and that he is God's new King. He has told his soldiers to find Jesus and kill him. Take Mary and Jesus far away to the land of Egypt and wait there until God tells you it is safe."

The angel disappeared and Joseph woke up. His heart was beating fast. He knew that they were in great danger and had to leave quickly.

Joseph led the way out of the little town and into the hills. As they climbed higher along the road that would lead them to Egypt, they could hear shouting in the streets below. Mary and Joseph looked back. They could see the flames of torches, held by Herod's soldiers. They were searching the houses looking for the baby King.

But Jesus was safe and sleeping soundly in Mary's arms.

She and Joseph knew that they would not be returning to their home in Nazareth for a long time.

— ☆ —

Joseph, Mary and Jesus spent many years in Egypt. Then, one day Joseph fell asleep and had another strange dream with a message from God. King Herod was dead. It was safe for them to return home.

Mary and Joseph bought a small horse and cart to carry them and their belongings back to Nazareth.

The journey took many weeks. But finally the little family drove into town. Joseph stopped the cart outside one of the houses. He got down and knocked at the door.

— ☆ —

A man answered. It was Mary's cousin Jacob.

"Joseph! Mary! Is that you?" shouted Jacob excitedly.

Other people came to see what was happening. Very soon, family and friends had all crowded round to welcome Joseph and Mary and to meet their son Jesus.

Mary and Joseph's journey had ended back in Nazareth, where the Christmas story first started.

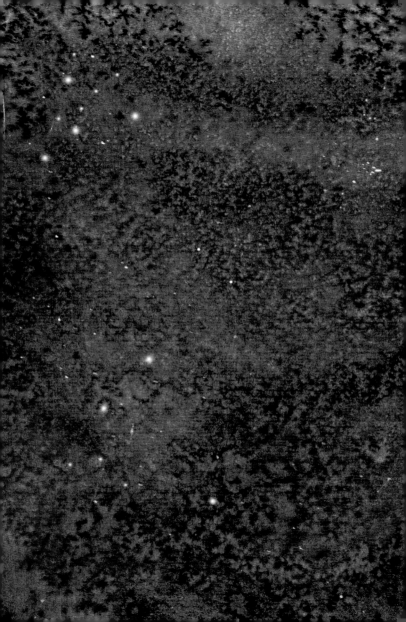